What Others are ?
LINKED Quick (

"As a Certified Personality Trainer who has used this priceless resource to help my business, marriage, and life coaching clients for many years, I am excited about the LINKED program. Through simple and practical assessments, as well as true stories, authors Linda Gilden and Linda Goldfarb provide an excellent way for people to learn more about themselves, and the people they interact with. Do you want to improve your personal and professional relationships? Keep a copy of *LINKED Quick Guide to Personalities* close at hand."

~Anita Agers Brooks, Inspirational Business/Life Coach, International Speaker, and Award-Winning Author

A must-read! The *LINKED Quick Guide to Personalities* is an insightful game-changer to the way we all interact with others. This guide provides a simple, concise, and fun way to tackle understanding the personalities around you and the tools to interact well with others. Don't miss this terrific way to increase productivity and enjoyability of life and work.

Aaron M. Zook, Jr, Colonel, U.S. Army (Retired), Certified Advanced Personality Trainer, Award Winning Author and CEO, ZookBooks

When my husband and I discovered the *LINKED* personality teaching during our Parenting Awesome Kids,-

class our family interaction changed dramatically. I no longer treated my children with a cookie cutter parenting approach. I discovered their unique tendencies and emotional needs and chose to meet each one directly. We've moved from living at the end of our ropes to experiencing more peace and calm in our home.

Kelly Harris, Mother of two girls

I thought other people had problems that I needed to fix. Learning how my personality-bent naturally responded to others helped me interact in a more positive way at home and at work. I now consider the personalities when I communicate, lead, and interact with others. I encourage everyone to get the *LINKED Quick Guide to Personalities*; it's a relational game-changer.

Will Trueblood, Husband, Father, Camp Director at Echo Grove Camp and Retreat Center, SE Michigan

The *LINKED Quick Guide to Personalities* is uncomplicated; even the personality names are easy to say and remember. Using simple and clear descriptive words, this quick guide helps us understand our personalities and the personalities of those we come in contact with each day. As a marriage coach, I help my clients understand who God created them to be and to recognize the personality of their husbands and family members. Once we know the basics of the four personalities as provided in the *LINKED Quick Guide,* we can make adjustments to how we relate to others and thus heal our relationships.

Joyce Zook, Marriage Coach, Board Certified Biblical Counselor, Author, Speaker, and Advanced Personality Trainer

LINKED

QUICK GUIDE
TO
PERSONALITIES

Suzanne
We're linked
for life
Linda
Bothorth

Blessings as you
share your sweet
personality with
others—
With love
Linda
Gildem

LINKED

QUICK GUIDE TO PERSONALITIES

Maximizing Life Connections
One Link at a Time

Linda Gilden and Linda Goldfarb

Bold Vision Books
PO Box 2011
Friendswood, Texas 77549

Dedication

To our readers—May God bless your journey of self-discovery through the personalities.

Table of Contents

Foreword

Transformation. That's exactly what happened when I learned about the personalities. It changed every area of my life. Over the last 30 years, I have educated men, women, and teens about the personalities and witnessed those "aha" moments when people actually "get it." Marriages have been saved, parents finally understand how to communicate with their children, professional careers become far more successful, and students interact with their teachers more effectively.

With years of experience in many walks of life, Gilden and Goldfarb are Advanced Personality Trainers who have not just taught these principles, they have lived them out day by day. Now they have taken their experiences, put them on paper and are bringing this wisdom to you so that you too can live your life more fully.

This *LINKED Quick Guide to Personalities* takes the authors' many years of study and development and pares it down to provide the reader with a concise reference guide that will give the information you need at just the moment you need it. Don't just get this guide. Use it. It will change your life.

Gerry Wakeland
Writer, speaker, and
women's ministry consultant

Introduction

Do you know people who are different from you? Do those differences bother you? Have you considered whether or not those *differences* could change based on *your* perspective? They can. It's the *perceived* motives behind the actions of others that often prevent relationships from growing, simply because you do not understand why they do what they do.

Each of us are different, created with unique personalities that influence our actions and reactions.

We can't control the actions of others. But we can control how we respond to them. Romans 12:18 says, "If it is possible, as far as it depends on you, live at peace with everyone." The key phrase is in the middle — "as far as it depends on you." We have a responsibility in our relationships — personal, family, business, or casual — to do everything we can to live peacefully. One of the core elements to living peacefully with others is understanding the personalities.

13

This LINKED Quick Guide, of self-discovery helps you understand your personality and the personalities of those around you. When you understand why you do the things you do and that they are a result of your God-given personality traits and your life experiences, your life connections will be strengthened one link at a time.

Connecting with others through the personalities opens the door to greater opportunities in every aspect of your life. Family, friends, coworkers, and even strangers will benefit from your new found perception. These are the four basic personality types we cover in LINKED.

Mobilizer

Get-it-done

Socializer

Life-of-the-party

Stabilizer

Keep-it-peaceful

Organizer

Everything-in-order

You may be familiar with these personality types by other names. Hippocrates called them choleric, sanguine, phlegmatic, and melancholy based on an interpretation of body fluids. Others have given them animal names such as lion, otter, golden retriever, and beaver. Then you have those who use terms such as upholder, obliger, questioner, and rebel or letters such as DISC.

This *LINKED Quick Guide to Personalities* uses the words Mobilizer, Socializer, Stabilizer, and Organizer. In every method of assessment there is a powerful personality, a playful personality, a peaceful personality, and a purposeful personality. No matter what you call them, each of the four corresponds with one of these descriptions.

Who needs a *LINKED Personality Quick Guide?*

- Anyone who values relationships and wants to make them stronger.

- Busy people who don't have time for intense studies about personalities.

- Individuals who desire information in a nutshell.

- People who engage with people on a regular basis—teachers, parents, employers, life coaches, pretty much everyone.

Why does understanding personalities work?

- Because people need people, and all people are not alike.

- Everyone has met someone they don't get along with.

- Everyone has met someone who makes them happy.

- Everyone has met someone who makes them feel uncomfortable.

- Knowing why we respond to people differently can only strengthen our relationships. And who wouldn't like that?

The answer is no one. We're created for relationships. Man's first relationship was with God the Father. In fact, the reason we were created was to have a relationship with God. Today we interact with all of God's creation, and as we read earlier, it's suggested we get along with everybody.

Sounds wonderful on paper, yet it takes intentionality. Finding out about yourself, how you relate to others, and meshing your personalities to create relationships that last—takes work.

"Personality has power to uplift,
power to depress, power to curse,
and power to bless."
~Paul Harris

Identify Your Personality
(who you are)

You may have heard about personalities for many years. Perhaps, you've never had the opportunity to know what personality you are and how it applies to your relationships. It only takes a few minutes to determine what your dominant personality is. The best way to figure it out is to take the LINKED Personality Assessment below.

Circle the answers that describe how you react most often. Go with your first thought, be as honest as you can, and don't over think your answers. For best results, don't answer thinking, "Is this a good or bad choice?" Mark one answer per question.

1. **You've been assigned a project to complete in two weeks. You**
   a. Get it done right away, even if you have to stay up late
   b. Procrastinate but finish well at the last minute
   c. Have a challenge finishing as you want the project perfect
   d. Take your time, finishing at an easy pace

2. **Friends would describe you as**
   a. Bold and to the point
   b. Fun and entertaining

    c.   Witty and detail-oriented

    d.   Likable and easy going

3. You find yourself in a conversation with neighbors or coworkers. You

    a.   Laugh sometimes and enjoy joining in

    b.   Listen and contribute only when needed

    c.   Might interrupt with a solution for most problems

    d.   Listen and offer encouragement

4. The most important thing to have in life is

    a.   Peace

    b.   Perfection

    c.   Fun

    d.   Control

5. When it comes to friends, you

    a.   Make friends easily

    b.   Have little need for friends

    c.   Make friends cautiously

    d.   Get along with everyone

6. When choosing a place to eat, you

    a.   Act spontaneously

    b.   Change your mind often

    c.   Have particular places in mind

    d.   Don't have a preference

7. **Your ideal weekend would include**
   a. Traveling to a new place
   b. Having quality time with your spouse or a friend
   c. Learning a new skill
   d. Having a pajama day

8. **When you are stressed, you**
   a. Find a quiet place to rest
   b. Call a friend and go shopping
   c. Get away to a spot where you're alone and can recharge
   d. Exercise more

9. **If you look in your closet you will see**
   a. All the hangers turned the same way and clothes neatly hung
   b. Bright colors and fun patterns
   c. Trendy outfits with all pieces hanging together
   d. A lot of comfortable clothes

10. **When your child is hurting, you**
   a. Cry with him or her
   b. Wrap your arms around him or her in a big hug
   c. Tell him or her to be strong and get back into life
   d. Try to make him or her feel better by planning something fun

11. When you are in a crowd, you

   a. Enjoy all your new best friends
   b. Wish you could hurry up and get home and put your feet up
   c. Retreat to the perimeter to talk to someone you already know
   d. Work the crowd to identify contacts

12. People often say you are

   a. Controlling
   b. Fun-loving
   c. Encouraging
   d. Laid back

13. Driving to work, you see a man knock a lady over and then, flee. You would most likely

   a. Call the police and jump to the lady's aid
   b. Park the car, call police, and wait
   c. Pass on by hoping she's okay
   d. Ask if she is alright and text friends to tell what you saw

14. Getting on an elevator to go four floors, you

   a. Waste no time in starting a conversation with those already on
   b. Move to the back corner and hope the elevator is fast
   c. Smile and stand quietly
   d. Push the button for your floor and ask the others which floor they're on

15. When unexpected company knocks at your door, you

a. Turn around and shout "Party!"
b. Invite them in and immediately begin tidying up
c. Tell them it's good to see them, but you have a headache
d. Invite them in, control the short visit, then stand and bid them good-bye

16. While lying in the hammock by the lake, you

a. Take a nap easily
b. Make a check-list for errands
c. Invite a friend to join you
d. Have a hard time just lying there

17. Your parents are coming for a visit. You

a. Rush around making sure everything is in place and clean
b. Brief the family on how to act and what to do
c. Decide the house is clean enough
d. Call all the relatives letting them know about the visit

18. When given the choice you prefer

a. To lead
b. To serve
c. To research
d. To entertain

19. When you are sad, you
  a. Read a book
  b. Tell a friend
  c. Work on a project
  d. Take a nap

20. When given the opportunity to voice your opinion
  a. You speak right up
  b. Give your opinion and more
  c. Choose your words carefully
  d. You say very few words

21. If you were a piece of a puzzle, you would be
  a. The corners
  b. The bright flowers
  c. The straight edges
  d. The background

22. In life, you tend to be
  a. Playful
  b. Purposeful
  c. Powerful
  d. Peaceful

23. Your car of choice would be
  a. Economical and safe
  b. Comfortable and easy to maintain
  c. Sporty and fun
  d. Stylish and dependable

24. You are drawn to
    a.   Things done the right way
    b.   Things done the fast way
    c.   Things done the easy way
    d.   Things done the fun way

25. Which word describes you best at home?
    a.   Competitive
    b.   Cautious
    c.   Committed
    d.   Carefree

26. Your co-workers describe you as
    a.   Results-oriented
    b.   Service-oriented
    c.   Detail-oriented
    d.   Pleasure-oriented

"I think it's my personality to overcome things, learn from them and become stronger, both personally and professionally. To be honest, I welcome those hardships."

~Hope Solo - Athlete

Linking Your Chain

This is your first step in discovering more about who you are. Circle your answers on the Assessment Key in the back of the book and record the numbers there. Transfer your totals below on the line designated by the name.

_____ Mobilizer

_____ Socializer

_____ Stabilizer

_____ Organizer

The highest total is your dominant personality. The next highest total is your secondary personality. Write them in the spaces on the next page.

Dominant   _____

Secondary   _____

Please note: You may find yourself in several categories and wonder if you are really just too mixed up to be anything. The answer is a resounding NO! God made each of us different for a reason. Some are no assessment needed, hands-down one personality, while others may exhibit characteristics of more than one. But for the most part, you will have a dominant personality.

Let's take a look at each personality and connect the links.

You might be a MOBILIZER if…

- You love to do things the fast way.

- You're a gifted leader who loves challenges.

- You tend to be focused, direct, and to the point.

- You demand loyalty and appreciation.

- You're distracted/disturbed when life is out of control.

- You like having your hands in several projects.

- Exercise and hard work relaxes you.

Mobilizers are the movers and shakers of the world. They set their goals and then move full speed ahead to accomplish them. Mobilizers make great leaders. You often see them as committee chairmen or heads of companies. If you want something done, the Mobilizer is a good choice for making that happen.

"Learning that I was a Mobilizer changed my life," says Chris. "People called me bossy, but I didn't understand why. The biggest thing I noticed was in my relationship with God. I have always wanted to be the one in charge, so it was hard for me to let Him take over my life. But, little by little, I have learned to depend on Him and that has truly been a life-changer in many ways."

Quick Tip for Mobilizers

Though you like to get things done quickly, remember not everyone works at your speed.

You might be a SOCIALIZER if...

- You love to do things the fun way.

- You're creative and a storyteller.

- You tend to speak a lot.

- You enjoy attention and approval.

- You're distracted/disturbed when life is no longer fun.

- You like freed up schedules and to be showered with affection.

- Eating out and/or shopping relaxes you.

Socializers love a party and seek the fun element in everything they do. Socializers love people and feel very lonely when they are not around them. Quiet time is difficult and often requires great discipline for the Socializer personality.

"I am often called the 'party girl' by my friends," says Lucy. "But sometimes I want to be more focused than that and it is really hard. I finally learned that if I made a list on my whiteboard each morning of the things I wanted to accomplish, I was a lot more likely to get things done. It's still not easy, and I often have to promise myself lunch with a friend as a reward for checking something off my list. Makes me feel good when I can do that."

Quick Tip for Socializers

Though you love fun, remember not
everyone is ready to party.

You might be a STABILIZER if…

- You love to do things the easy way.

- You tend to think before you speak.

- You appreciate respect and like feeling worthy.

- You're supportive, easy going, and work well under pressure.

- You like peace and quiet.

- You're distracted/disturbed when life is chaotic.

- Time alone such as watching TV or reading a book relaxes you.

Stabilizers are seen as the quiet and relaxed personality. Other personalities often wish they could live that way. Stabilizers love people yet shy away from conflict and change. This personality enjoys situations where they don't feel pressure or stress.

Will says, "Growing up, my family called me lazy, and I believed them. They never understood that I really loved doing things with them; I just didn't like doing them at the same pace. Knowing I am a Stabilizer has helped me to understand that my slower pace is okay. Now, family time is more enjoyable because I can be myself."

Quick Tip for Stabilizers

Though you enjoy taking life nice and easy, remember not everyone keeps a slower pace.

You might be an ORGANIZER if...

- You love to do things the right way.

- You're loyal and sensitive.

- You tend to listen more, speak less, and think a lot.

- You're thoughtful and deliberate.

- You're distracted/disturbed when life is imperfect.

- You like quality over quantity.

- Long stretches of silence and plenty of space relaxes you.

Organizers are rule followers who often get labeled as perfectionists. Those with this personality may also find it hard to love unconditionally. As a deep thinker, the Organizer is often well-grounded in his or her faith. If you need a good listener, the Organizer is probably your person.

Anna says, "When I discovered that my perfectionist tendencies were a personality trait and not an inborn desire to drive myself and everyone around me crazy, it was liberating. I allowed myself the freedom to be who God created me to be. I quit imposing my perfectionism on others, especially my family. I was free to accept friends for the way they were. It wasn't an overnight thing but as I worked at it, I began to enjoy relationships without the encumbrance of judgment."

Quick Tip for Organizers

Though you may be right, remember
others can be right, too.

"I've always had a duck personality. Calm above water, feet going crazy below."

~K. Flay - Musician

Internalize How You Relate To Others

Now you know who you are by identifying your dominant personality. Let's take a quick look at how your personality relates to others.

 If you are a Mobilizer:

People sometimes want to label you as "bossy." The truth is, you're task-oriented and like control. If you see a situation you can improve by jumping in and directing the actions of everyone else, you do it. Be aware of this tendency and instead of jumping in uninvited, ask if you can help.

You also like to create a check list so you can progress toward a goal. This is a great idea. Just don't be too stringent about others helping you complete your list. That will likely not be an issue for you, however, because you sometimes have difficulty delegating jobs to others. You like knowing it will be done the way you like and how better for that to happen than for you to do it yourself.

You're a great leader and in leadership positions you excel. You will work tirelessly to make sure you do a good job.

 *If you are a Socializer:*

You use your love of people to encourage and help them enjoy life. Be careful though, as a people-friendly person, you can overwhelm other personalities with your upbeat high-energy.

Understand that you may have trouble staying on task when you're working on a project. Set up a schedule of mini-rewards (phone chat with a friend, browsing through an online catalog, etc) along the way to keep yourself on track.

Never try to squelch your vibrant, fun-loving personality. Many people wish they could be as extroverted as you are.

 *If you are a Stabilizer:*

You have great ideas but seldom share them because of your introverted tendency. Speak up.

Don't be content to sit in the background and let others do all the talking. You have something important to say.

Understand that God made you to be less intense in many ways than other people. Enjoy it. Don't let someone else's conflict get in the way of your peace. You are the peacemaker, and in being that way, you tend to be a fast and loyal friend.

Stabilizers are easy to get along with and make great team players.

If you are an Organizer:

Being task-oriented, you'll have to make an extra effort to hang out and socialize with friends. Sometimes it's just too much, as you really prefer being alone. Deep down you enjoy your friends and want to build those relationships. It's not as easy for you as your Socializer and Stabilizer friends.

You're a great listener and people often gravitate to you with their problems. Your advice is usually well-grounded and rooted in your faith. You accomplish much because of your attention to detail and deadline.

Ask questions, to make sure you understand any part of a conversation you're unsure about. You easily get your feelings hurt because of your sensitivity and many times it's the result of just not clarifying what another person says.

No Matter Your Personality:
Embrace the full concept of "as far
as it depends on me," and understand no
matter what personality you are, you have
control over your perspective and how
you interact with others.

"I think it's part of my personality
—I love to travel; I love different
cultures and philosophies and
perspectives on things."
~Martin Henderson - Actor

Key Word Identifiers

Here are a few more key word identifiers to help you connect with your personality better.

Extrovert
Fast-Responder

Mobilizer

Not Easily Discouraged
Delegates
Independent
Leader
Courageous
Results-oriented
Straightforward
Competitive
Controlling
Decisive
Loves a Challenge

Socializer

Doesn't Hold Grudges
Touchy Feely
Enthusiastic
Colorful Dresser
People-oriented
Optimistic
Spontaneous
Volunteers
Talkative
Disorganized
Seeks Social Acceptance

Introvert
Slow-Responder

Organizer

Stays Behind the Scenes
Detail-oriented
Self-disciplined
Cautious
Analytical
Pessimistic
Neat and Tidy
Compassionate
Tends to Be Right
Doesn't Make Friends Easily
Loves Charts, Tables, and
Graphs

Stabilizer

Hides Emotions
Indecisive
Service-oriented
Humble
Committed
Steadfast
Team Player
Patient
Low-Key
Supportive
Easy to Get Along With

Noting the additional words extrovert and fast-responding between the Mobilizer and Socializer, both of these personalities share these behavior styles but for different reasons. The Mobilizer gains control by his or her extrovert trait while the Socializer gains attention; and the fast-responding Mobilizer, though meticulous, prefers to check off boxes quickly while the free-spirited Socializer is found to be very spontaneous moving from one thought to another quickly.

Organizers and Stabilizers keep to themselves as introverts. Time spent behind the scenes by himself is pleasing to the Stabilizer; while the Organizer doesn't require the input of others to complete her tasks. The term slow-responding in no fashion relates to the mental prowess of these two personalities; the Organizer takes her time because she's into the details and research before giving her opinion, while the Stabilizer is fairly laid back and okay with others making decisions. He doesn't get riled up. When he says things are fine, he truly means it.

Remember, this is a *Quick Guide to Personalities.* As such, there may be more questions you want answered. Please don't hesitate to ask us your questions; we love connecting with our readers. You will find our contact information at the back of this book.

"Always be yourself, express yourself, have faith in yourself, do not go out and look for a successful personality and duplicate it."
~Bruce Lee - Martial Arts/Actor

Implement What You
Have Learned

Now that you know who you are and why you do what you do, let's put it to use in your daily relationships.

Implementing the full value of the personalities, to enhance your relationships, requires knowing what your strengths and weaknesses are as well as those of others. Having that basic understanding, you will know what the potential areas of conflict are and how to avoid them. You will also know how to approach friends and family in the best way possible to grow your relationship.

For example, Wanda is a very strong Socializer mother who always wants to be around people. She can turn every opportunity into a party. She and her Socializer daughter, Emily, often plan fun things with the whole family. However, middle child, Greg, is very much an Organizer. Most of the things Emily and her mother think are fun seem frivolous to him. How can they get along as a family and find common ground for making memories they all can enjoy?

As Wanda, Emily, and Greg became aware of the different personalities in their family, it helped them come to a compromise. While fun and engaging activities are what the girls need and want, Greg prefers activities that are more subdued, intellectual, and enriching., they compromise. Family vacation plans now include a theme park for the girls and an afternoon at the museum for Greg.

Wanda and her family strengthened their connections with each other by putting their personality knowledge into action. Read on for more quick-tips to help you link your personality to others.

Linking Personality to Personality

Interacting with the personalities of the people you know can result in a positive or negative way based on how you approach others. Read through the following connecting considerations to better the chance of your relationships moving forward in a positive direction.

Mobilizers Connecting

With Other Mobilizers

 Understand the need for other Mobilizers you work with to be in charge. But if you are indeed, the head person on a project, find another area you can ask the Mobilizers on your team to handle. By putting them in charge, it will be done well. This is where you put your delegation into action.

With Socializers

 Your Socializer friends and you are very different. You tend to have blinders on

51

as you move toward your goal in the fastest and most efficient way possible. If you're working with Socializers, realize they will lose interest in working with you very quickly if some part of the project is not fun and lively.

Compliment freely. When texting, it's best to use fun emojis to assure the Socializer you're not mad. Seriously! Even though the Socializer appears self-secure, deep down they crave knowing they're appreciated and loved.

With Stabilizers

Using a few warm and fuzzy words will go a long way with Stabilizers. Your abrupt way of moving single-focused toward your goals may appear tactless, harsh and uncaring. Therefore, slow down and focus on the person, not the goal. Smiling more shows you're interested in what they have to say.

Stabilizers are excellent support people; they can take on many roles, but don't overwhelm them. Think slow and steady.

With Organizers

Remember Organizers tend to be sensitive. They also process at a slower pace than you do. When working toward a goal, you may tend to overlook Organizers as possible helpers because they're quiet. But Organizers are great project helpers because of their researching skills and time management.

Organizers need to be praised for their part in the project or they won't feel appreciated. Praise is not something you give freely. So make an effort to praise those working with you.

Socializers Connecting

With Mobilizers

Remember Mobilizers are get-to-the-point, no-nonsense people who just want the facts. A very short story with a strong take away may work for them but otherwise, just give them the straight information. Don't embellish, don't string it out, just tell it like it is.

Mobilizers always have the goal in mind. Therefore, they will ask, *What are we trying to accomplish here?* Honor their personality by helping them find new ways to get there. You're a creative thinker and may come up with solutions the Mobilizer never considered.

With Other Socializers

Remember you both can't be center stage. If you're in a group situation and there are several other Socializers, you can't all be the life of the party at one time. Be respectful of the needs of the other Socializers there. You should understand them better than anyone else.

Find something to praise your Socializer friends about. Though you enjoy the attention yourself, a word of praise to a fellow Socializer goes a long way in filling their love tank.

With Stabilizers

Stabilizers can be your best friends. The Stabilizers' calm and cool personality can help Socializers remain grounded in the moment. You both enjoy being around people but respond differently to them.

Don't expect too much of your Stabilizer friends as far as activity goes. They'll want to participate and join you on some of your escapades but then will need to regroup and refresh with moments of rest and quiet.

With Organizers

Organizers like to think through every response and process every bit of new information. Give them time to do that. You're spontaneous and they're methodical, seeing things in a totally different light.

Organizers may also be slow to respond to your jokes. Don't force it, just let it be. And, while you find a way to make everything fun, remember Organizers have to work at having a good time.

Stabilizers Connecting

With Mobilizers

The goal-oriented Mobilizer could be a source of stress for you when in his or her presence for long periods of time. But it needn't be.

Find ways to digest the ways and direction of the Mobilizer and compensate for your difference by finding ways you can help him or her reach a goal.

In conversation with a Mobilizer keep conversations short and to the point. Remember, they really don't like all the details that fascinate you.

With Socializers

You will enjoy the energy and flashiness of the Socializer but if you spend a lot of time around him or her, you will get tired just by observing. Make the most of your time together then go rest.

Every once in a while give in to the invitations of your Socializer friends to go out in a group. Your love of people will surface and you will be appreciated.

With Other Stabilizers

Stabilizer to Stabilizer is a fast friend combination. They are easy going and really enjoy each other's company because what they expect from the friendship is a goal they can both attain. Enjoy the relaxation of just being with someone who "gets" you.

With Organizers

Organizers will love your willingness to help in all situations. They will love having you on their committees and they will love the challenge to keep you motivated and involved.

Even though the perception of Organizers is perfectionists, they don't expect it from everyone without work. If you are working with an Organizer, don't hesitate to ask questions. He or she will appreciate that you want to do things correctly and will help you reach a level of understanding to do so.

Organizers Connecting

With Mobilizers

You share an attention to detail and deadlines with the Mobilizer. But his/her drive to the finish line may outshine your love of research and depth. When working with Mobilizers, find an area that requires your skills and volunteer to put them to work.

Don't take everything personally. Sometimes the abrupt nature of the Mobilizers makes you feel unimportant and uncared for. Understand they are fast-paced and bullet-point focused. It really isn't personal.

With Socializers

You may feel inclined to roll your eyes at the energy and frivolity of the Socializer. Get over that and they will become your fast friends. You often wish you could just let go and participate in their fun excursions but it's really hard for you to do.

Your creative side loves to get together and brainstorm with the Socializers because of their energy.

But remember, you thrive on time alone. If you've been in the company of Socializers for an extended period of time, attending a party, etc. you will most likely need some time alone to recharge your batteries.

With Stabilizers

Always communicate to the Stabilizers around you how important they are to you and how much you appreciate them. Never overwhelm a Stabilizer friend with too many decisions at one time. Give them space and lots of time to contemplate their decisions.

Allow them the freedom to be who they are and work in the manner they choose. Don't be surprised by frequent breaks and the need for a little solitude.

With Other Organizers

You probably work well with other Organizers. You'll agree on the need for detail and depth. Just be sure you understand your assignment and the exact outcome expected.

Two perfectionists working on a project could also mean the project never gets done. Lay aside the perfectionism to focus on working together for the end goal.

"I am what is mine. Personality is the original personal property."
~Norman O. Brown - Philosopher

Where and When to Use Your Knowledge of the LINKED Personalities

Short answer to when and where to use your knowledge of the LINKED Personalities—everywhere and all day long.

Many times during the day I'm surprised by an action or reaction of those around me. That is, until I realize the behavior that dominated was the result of strong personality characteristics.

For instance, one area of the country experienced a total eclipse of the sun not too long ago.

The Socializers were thrilled and began making plans for parties. When the day came, if they had not thought enough ahead to plan, they gathered a group of friends and quickly put together a party for this monumental event. The news showed scores of eclipse parties in backyards, parks, fields, lakes, and the like. It was a party day and the nation was excited.

But what about the other personalities? How did they link themselves to this event?

The Mobilizers could very well have decided to gather friends together. But they decided way before the date, had it planned in every way, and specified this was a get together to watch the eclipse and when the eclipse was over the party was over.

The Organizers were busy making sure everyone had their special glasses well ahead of time and they were the correct ISO number so as not to injure the eyes. After securing the glasses, they made sure that everyone knew how important it was to have the glasses and instructed them on how to use them.

The Stabilizers were well aware of the event and its importance in history. They were excited to be part of the events others had planned. Many may have put off buying their glasses until the last minute and were hoping the party host would provide them.

Another consideration is how we prepare to take trips. Understanding the personalities make packing, preparation, and participation a lot smoother. Listen to Marcia's story.

Marcia traveled to see her sister in another state. Marcia wanted to make sure everything went according to plan. She had laid her clothes out the night before. Her suitcases were packed and her boarding pass on top. She knew what she would eat for breakfast, when she would eat it, and what time they would need to leave.

The morning of her flight, Marcia got ready. With thirty minutes to spare she began asking her husband,

"Are you ready to go?"

"Not quite, honey. But last night you said you wanted to leave the house at 10:25. It is only 9:55. I'll be ready by 10:25. I just need to call Gerald and set up our golf game for Saturday. I'll be ready to put your suitcase in the car shortly."

"Shortly? My suitcase has been ready since last night."
"I know sweetheart and I'll have it in the car in plenty of time. I'll be ready to go."

Marcia went back into the bedroom to check and make sure the boarding pass was still on the suitcase. She checked her purse to make sure she had sunglasses, snacks, and makeup.

She finally went into the kitchen pretending to get a drink of water but really checking to see where her husband was. She found him looking through yesterday's mail. He was browsing through the newest cycling magazine.

"Foster, I am going to miss my plane! You will have time to read your magazine while I am gone."

"I doubt it, honey. Tonight I am eating with some guys. Then after the golf game tomorrow Martin and I are going to see a movie. I had to make a few notes to remember what I am doing when. You know I am not really a note person but I don't want to miss anything."

"Doesn't sound like you are going to miss me at all. But, speaking of missing, I really don't want to miss my plane. Would you please help me get my things into the car?"

Do you relate to either of these characters? Based on your personality, what would you do in that situation? _____

_____

_____

_____

_____

_____

_____

Because Marcia is an Organizer, she wanted everything ready and in order for her trip—not just on time but early. She had been planning for days so she wouldn't be rushed or late. Every item on her list had been carefully packed and she knew exactly where it was. She had even bought surprises for her niece and nephews.

Her husband, on the other hand, is a Socializer. His preparation and exit from the house would be much different than Marcia's. Packing his suitcase would not concern him until the last minute and then it would be a frenzy with very little pre-planning. He may not have packed every little thing, but he would buy what he needed at his destination and enjoy the trip just the same.

Hugh's Story

Hugh was working his way up the corporate ladder. He arrived at work on time each morning dressed in a clean white shirt and pressed red tie. He spoke to each of his superiors matter-of-factly, in a way that let them know he was ready to get down to business.

The day of his important presentation arrived and his routine was the same. He was ready. He had gone over his checklist numerous times and knew his material. His confident step sent the message, *This is going to be a cinch*. Hugh went to the break room to get his coffee and made it just the way he did every day—half a sugar packet and a squirt of milk. Hugh gave it a stir and whistled as he started toward the door.

Just as he rounded the corner, Mazie ran right into Hugh. Splat! The entire cup of coffee went all over his crisply starched white shirt.

"Oh, I am so sorry," Mazie grabbed a handful of napkins from the counter. "I was looking at my notes for the meeting and wasn't paying attention." She offered Hugh the napkins.

Hugh raised his hands. "I'll take care of it, Mazie. You are always in a dream world. Just look up once in a while."

"Can I take your shirt to the cleaners? Something? I know you have a big presentation soon."

"No, just be more careful. You should always pause before you come around a corner like that." Hugh started toward the door. He turned back to Mazie. "Actually, you can do something. Just fix me another cup of coffee, please. Half a sugar and a squirt of milk. Bring it to my office carefully and set it on my desk. I always keep another shirt in the office in case I need a quick change."

"Thank you. I'll be right up with your coffee—and, yes, I'll be careful."

How would you react in that situation? Are you more like Hugh or Mazie? Record your reaction here.

_____

_____

_____

_____

_____

_____

Hugh's matter-of-fact Mobilizer personality did not welcome Mazie's distracted behavior. He really didn't have time for this kind of interruption but because he was totally prepared for his presentation and armed with a change of clothes, no major damage was done.

Mazie's low-key Stabilizer personality set her up for this unexpected collision with her boss. Embarrassed, Mazie recovered and spent the rest of the day in her cubicle, completing her work at her usual steady pace.

The Twins' Story

Sarah and Morgan were twins. Everyone expected them to be just alike. But that wasn't exactly true of these sisters. Here's a bit about them.

Super Socializer Sarah couldn't wait for the weekend to get there. She and Morgan were going to a surprise birthday party for their cousin. On the other hand, Morgan dreaded going to the party. Morgan's Organizer personality could think of a hundred, no probably a thousand, places she would rather go on Friday night.

When they arrived at the party, Morgan hung behind Sarah. Sarah entered the door, eyes roving in search of a friend. With a wave, a backward nod, and a hasty, "You don't mind, do you, Morg?" Sarah was off to join a chattering group of friends.

Morgan was used to this. Glancing around the room to find a friend, she soon spotted Aggie over by the drink table. Aggie was getting some punch alone and Morgan knew she had already found an out-of-the-way spot to sit and would return with her punch. Morgan followed Aggie to the bench on the other side of the table.

Sarah went from friend group to friend group. She was laughing and talking and obviously enjoying herself. She and her equally Socializer friends often talked all at once. Even from a distance you could see them admiring new shoes or a new outfit.

At the end of the evening, Sarah and Morgan chatted on the way home.

"Wasn't that the best party ever, Morg?" Sarah asked.

"Well, it was pretty much like—"

Sarah interrupted her sister, "I knew you would agree. There were so many great people there. I'm glad you had a good time, too."

"But, I—"

"I know. I knew you would have a good time once you got there."

How do you feel about being part of large group gatherings? Do you identify more with Sarah or

Morgan? If you are like Sarah, what steps have you taken to include those you are close to in parties you enjoy? If you are more like Morgan, how have you made yourself more comfortable in large group situations?

_____

_____

_____

_____

_____

_____

Sarah always thrives in a crowd. Her Socializer personality makes her the life of the party. No one is a stranger to Sarah.

Morgan's Organizer personality does not enjoy large, group events. Her idea of a fun evening is curling up with a good book in front of a cozy fire.

Dinner Table Conversation

George sat at the end of the table. He hadn't said much, but he smiled at the appropriate times and even shared a chuckle now and then. He ate his food, pausing between bites to sit back in his chair. Others at the table were talking and laughing with each other, deep in conversation.

About halfway through the meal Sue turned to George and said, "What do you think? You've been awfully quiet."

"I totally agree with Brandon. But, I would like to suggest a new option…" George had been perfectly comfortable in his position as listener all the while contemplating how he would contribute to the conversation when the opportunity came.

The conversation continued through dinner. George enjoyed the evening and felt just as much part of the group as those he was dining with. Others didn't always understand George's Stabilizer personality but they appreciated his calm easy going manner and the wisdom he contributed to the conversations when he chose to join in.

Can you identify with George? Or are one of the others at the table always vying for a spot in the conversation?

_____

_____

_____

_____

_____

_____

George loves people. He enjoys getting to know them but prefers one-on-one conversations. In a situation like the dinner table above, George felt part of the dinner even though his interaction was minimal. George's peaceful Stabilizer personality puts him at ease in many situations.

Lasting Links to Everyday Life

As we wrap up, consider these final words of personality-specific encouragement:

Mobilizer

Delegate with love and appreciation

Temper your directness with a smile

Lead others with boldness and courage

Socializer

Enjoy your fun-loving ways

Lavish your love on people

Use good judgment when being spontaneous

Stabilizer

Be confident in volunteering your services

Find another steadfast friend to relax with

Use your patience to manage conflict among others

Organizer

Temper your perfectionist bent with humility

Allow others freedom to be themselves

Reach out to others and cultivate friendships

We pray this quick guide has equipped you with information you can put to use today.

Check out the following Q & A and let us know what other questions you have.

Q & A with the Authors

Q—Why do you think a study of the personalities is so important?

A—Knowing your personality frees you to be the person God created you to be. It's human nature to compare yourself to others. Children often look up to someone and you hear them say, "I want to be Superman when I grow up."

God didn't make everyone to be Superman. Once you realize God made you to be you; you are free to be the best you that you can be.

Understanding the personalities of others allows you to interact and link with them in a way that allows them to be who God made them to be and you to accept them as such. You no longer pass judgment on others because they are not just like you. You realize they have strengths and weaknesses and want to help them maximize their strengths.

Q—At what age does a person's personality become obvious to others?

A—Some will argue there is no way to determine personalities at a young age. However, once you are aware of the characteristics of the different personalities, you realize some traits begin to exhibit themselves in infancy and toddlerhood.

Observing children at play, I'm sure you've noticed some play together well and some don't. The way in which they play is telling as well. Sarah dumps her blocks out in a pile by turning the bucket over. Kyle takes each block out of the bucket one by one and strategically place them on the floor. Rebecca arranges hers in a creative pattern while, Justin, doesn't seem to care how they are arranged. Based on their God-given nature, children are Socializers, Mobilizers, Organizers, and Stabilizers.

Q—How can all this information make a difference in my workplace? We all have to get the job done.

A—Knowing the personalities of your coworkers allows you to work with them and link them to the best possible position for them. If you are supervising a group of people, knowing their work styles allows you to match them to the best possible assignments. When you are able to do that, your office will run more smoothly and efficiently and you will have happier and more productive personnel.

For example, Miriam was a secretarial assistant and she was miserable. Spending all day long in an office where she rarely saw another person felt like torture. Once her boss learned the value of linking people to the right job personality-wise, Miriam became a different person. When the receptionist position came open, her boss moved Miriam to that position where she answered the phone and was hostess to all the business people waiting for appointments. This job was much better suited for Miriam's Socializer personality. Those who were waiting loved it as well because Miriam's social, yet professional personality made waiting much more pleasant.

Q—How does understanding the personalities impact my daily life?

A—Everyday we talk with people, whether in person or through technology. Think about the miscommunication that occurs when we speak. Most of it can be eliminated if we speak to the personality instead of the person.

Speaking to the personality of the person helps me, a Mobilizer, curb my reactions so I can consider a better path instead of my gut impression. I take a breath (albeit a second or two) and allow a response to come out, based on who they are and who I am, instead of words that could possibly ignite hurt feelings.

Q—So you're suggesting I consider the other person first?

A—Yes. God tells us we are to love others as we love ourselves, therefore considering the way another individual receives you is very important in linking together. You will find the seconds it takes to think of others first, will save you and them a lot of conflict. You may learn a bit more about their backstory as well.

Q—I have high numbers in two of the personality types, is that normal?

A—Absolutely. There is natural blending of the personalities; Mobilizer-Socializer, Socializer-Stabilizer, Stabilizer-Organizer, and Organizer-Mobilizer. In some cases, unnatural combinations occur that go against our design, as in Mobilizer-Stabilizer or Socializer-Organizer. These usually occur based on learned behavior resulting in the person assuming a personality that isn't his or her natural bent. If you fall into that category, please contact us, a coaching session would help greatly in clearing this up.

Be sure to visit www.LinkedPersonalities.com and www.facebook.com/linkedpersonalites for podcasts, teachings, and coaching opportunities.

Assessment Key

	Mobilizer	Socializer	Stabilizer	Organizer
1	a	b	d	c
2	a	b	d	c
3	c	a	d	b
4	d	c	a	b
5	b	a	d	c
6	c	a	d	b
7	c	a	d	b
8	d	b	a	c
9	c	b	d	a
10	c	d	b	a
11	d	a	b	c
12	a	b	d	c
13	a	d	c	b
14	d	a	c	b
15	d	a	c	b
16	b	c	a	d
17	b	d	c	a
18	a	d	b	c
19	c	b	d	a
20	a	b	d	c
21	a	b	d	c
22	c	a	d	b
23	d	c	b	a
24	b	d	c	a
25	a	d	c	b
26	a	d	b	c
Total				
	Mobilizer	Socializer	Stabilizer	Organizer

Meet the Authors

Linda Gilden

My introduction to the personalities came more than twenty years ago and was life-changing. On discovering that I was a purposeful, melancholy Organizer, I learned that perfectionism is one of my traits. I also learned that not only did I expect perfectionism of myself but of everyone around me. That was a real eye-opener. It helped me learn not to be so hard on myself or others. Once I understood my perfectionism I was free to be me and let others do the same. My relationships with friends and family improved dramatically as I allowed those around me to be who God intended them to be. Welcome to the exciting world of personalities. You are about to go on amazing journey.

Linda Gilden (Rose) - Author, Speaker, Writing Coach, Writer Conference Director, Certified Advanced Personalities Trainer and Consultant

Linda Goldfarb

My fifteen-year journey of studying and teaching the personalities has grown me as a powerful Mobilizer. I've learned to temper my pointing, soften my tone, and dress to be more inviting as a speaker. As a writer, I capture my audience's attention by using easy to understand words, adding stories, showing my research and always making a point. As a board certified Christian life coach I guide my clients, specific to their personalities, resulting in higher goals reached in a shorter timeframe. My personal relationships have grown to a deeper level as well. Now it's your turn. I hope you're ready to connect with others in ways you've never done before.

Linda Goldfarb (Goldie) - Author, International Speaker, Founder of Parenting Awesome Kids, Board Certified Advanced Life Coach, Certified Advanced Personalities Trainer and Consultant

Acknowledgments

We are so blessed to be able to share with you the *LINKED® Quick Guide to Personalities*. Knowing who God made us to be allows each of us to live freely and more fully in Him.

Thank you, Florence Littauer, Gerry Wakeland, and the CLASS family. Because of you we have an understanding of our personalities that has allowed us to build and grow relationships in a deeper way. Thank you.

To Bold Vision Books. What a blessing to work with such a professional team to whom only excellence will do. Thank you for believing that this project can change lives.

To our writers groups, Shawn and Suzanne Kuhn, and others who have brainstormed with us and shared ideas, thank you.

Jonathan Bishop, thank you for using your creativity to birth our emoji personality people.

Our families are our head cheerleaders. We love you and appreciate you. The sacrifices you have made for the writing of this book have not gone unnoticed.

Acknowledgments are never complete without recognizing the direction of the Creator of all. Thank You, God, for the opportunity to be Your messengers.

More LINKED PERSONALITY RESOURCES FOR YOU

Visit LINKEDPersonalities.com for more information and to order LINKED Personality Assessment.

Watch for more Quick Guides Coming Soon.

LINKED Quick Guide to Personalities for Parents
Maximizing Family Connections One Link at a Time

LINKED Quick Guide to Personalities for Educators
Maximizing Classroom Connections One Link at a Time

LINKED Quick Guide to Personalities for Writers
Maximizing Connections with Your Audience and Industry Professionals One Link at a Time

LINKED Quick Guide to Personalities for Leaders
Maximizing Relational Skills One Link at a Time

LINKED Quick Guide to Personalities for Teens
Maximizing Relationships One Link at a Time